love poems for
covenant keepers

Other Publications
* love poems for the natural woman
* The Believer's Guide to Christmas

Forthcoming Publications
* love poems for my mother
* love poems for my sisters
* love poems for my abba father
* love poems for girls from the ghetto
* love poems for family reunions
* love poems for the father I never knew
* love poems for the homeless christian

Workshops
* Cat Issues for Women
* Dog Issues for Men
* Grantwriting 101 and 102
* How to Start a Drama Ministry *(without the drama)*
* How to Serve Your Community *(with Agape Love)*
* The Crossroad *for Developing Evergreen Employees*

love poems for *covenant keepers*

Passion Writer
Donna Olds White

love poems for covenant keepers
Copyright © 2015 Donna Olds White
All rights reserved.

Come and Grow Communications Group, Inc.
111 S. Highland Street, Suite 331
Memphis, TN 38111

www.comeandgrowcommunicationsgroup.com

ISBN-13: 978-0692381199
ISBN-10: 0692381198

All rights reserved. Non-commercial interests may reproduce portions of this book provided the text does not exceed 500 words. When reproducing text from this book, the following must be included:

"*love poems for covenant keepers* Copyright © 2015 Donna Olds White Used by permission. All rights reserved."

Commercial use: No part of this publication may be reproduced, distributed, or transmitted in any form or by any means, except in the case of brief quotations embodied in critical reviews and certain other noncommercial uses permitted by copyright law.

Stream Poetry™ is an original trademark of Donna Olds White. All rights reserved.

Unless noted otherwise, all scripture is taken from the Holy Bible, New International Version®, NIV® Copyright © 1973, 1978, 1984, 2011 by Biblica, Inc.® Used by permission. All rights reserved worldwide.

Printed in the United States of America

Dedication

To Glenn and Brenda Manuel, my first and best close-up examples of marriage in real time for nearly 40 years!

To Dr. Sammie and Mrs. Addie Holloway, for teaching God's beautiful plan for marriage and officiating my wedding.

To Rodney and Ephie Johnson, for creating the LoveBuilders Program to strengthen marriages in the black community.

To all the couples who work daily to keep their covenant with God and each other.

And always I dedicate my writing to my mama, Louise the poet, who allowed her little girl to speak from the heart!

Why Love Poems?

If I speak in the tongues of men or of angels, but do not have love, I am only a resounding gong or a clanging cymbal. If I have the gift of prophecy and can fathom all mysteries and all knowledge, and if I have a faith that can move mountains, but do not have love, I am nothing. If I give all I possess to the poor and give over my body to hardship that I may boast, but do not have love, I gain nothing.

Love is patient, love is kind. It does not envy, it does not boast, it is not proud. It does not dishonor others, it is not self-seeking, it is not easily angered, it keeps no record of wrongs. Love does not delight in evil but rejoices with the truth. It always protects, always trusts, always hopes, always perseveres.

Love never fails. But where there are prophecies, they will cease; where there are tongues, they will be stilled; where there is knowledge, it will pass away.

For we know in part and we prophesy in part, but when completeness comes, what is in part disappears. When I was a child, I talked like a child. I thought like a child, I reasoned like a child. When I became a man, I put the ways of childhood behind me. For now we see only a reflection as in a mirror; then we shall see face to face. Now I know in part; then I shall know fully, even as I am fully known.

And now these three remain: faith, hope and love. But the greatest of these is love.
—1 Corinthians 13 NIV

Love never fails. When we start from a place of love, we can share anything, face anything, get through anything. Love is the river that brings life to all around it. Love is the calm in any storm. Love is a verb. Poems can capture experiences and emotions in a moment of time. They invite us to see and feel with our hearts what our heads may not understand or have time to process. It is my hope that these love poems will be a means by which we give time and consent for them to take us to the places that many of us need to go and remind us of the power of God that is within us to do anything but fail!

What's Inside

Acknowledgments	xi
Introduction	xiii
Time to Celebrate!	15
When the Sun is Shining	27
When the Rain is Falling	37
Time to Celebrate Again!	51
The Charge to Covenant Keepers	63
Before You Go…	69
About the PassionWriter	73

Acknowledgments

I wish to acknowledge with heartfelt thanks my mother, Louise Gwendolyn Olds, for giving me her gift of writing and poetry

My beautiful friend Emmabeth Weaver who, through her gentle words, basket of blessings and referral of Dell, provided the final push I needed to share what I have

To Dell Self, the book coach from heaven, who shared her knowledge with such love and expertise and more love

To all those (named and unnamed) whose marriages served as inspiration for many of my poems

To all who have spoken words of encouragement over many years

To Orcutt and Mathieu White, my husband and son, who love and support me daily in a million different ways

And to God, to Whom all the glory belongs for the things He has done!

Introduction

I never had a good idea of what it meant to be married until I was almost grown. I grew up in a home with one parent who did everything. I rarely saw her in affectionate relationships. I only knew a few married couples so I found it mysterious to think of what it must be like to be married.

As an adult, I decided that I didn't want to be married because it seemed to be too much work for the woman! All that cooking and cleaning and having babies? No thank you please! But then God set me on a path to meet a man from whom my heart couldn't hide. I loved him and wanted to be wherever he was, even if that was in Jamaica! In spite of distance and all other obstacles we married and so began my real-life experience of marriage!

This book of love poems came about as a result of seeing what God does through this miraculous union where two people become one flesh. It's more than regular sex and shared bills. Indeed it is a mystery! Every day He is teaching us how to love each other and this book is my way of sharing with you what I am learning. Blessings to every reader!

Time to Celebrate!

Marriage is not a fast knot, but a slip knot.

———

Two eyes see better than one.

———

Love is like a baby: it needs to be treated tenderly.

———

Let your love be like the misty rain, coming softly but flooding the river.

—African Proverbs

Time to Celebrate!

This Poem is for You	19
Let Us – Make a Memory	20
Ode to Valentine's Day	21
The House that Love Built	22
Anniversary Affirmation	23
Ode to My Cowboy	24

≈ denotes stream poetry

This Poem is for You

This poem is for all the LoveBuilders and love makers, for real-deal lovers who choose not to be fakers.

This is for those who come together because of and in spite of just to preserve the love and to communicate with their mate, enjoy a weekend date, knowing that it's never too late when

God is on your side.

This poem is for those who choose daily to stay in the game and run for the touchdown, even when it's 4th and 10, your team is behind and the 2-minute warning sounds.

This is for the Super Bowl that you play every day! Hey, you both already wear the ring! Now all that's left is to drink the champagne of this kingdom life!

So celebrate your husband, lady!

Husband, celebrate your wife!

This poem is for you!

Let Us — Make a Memory

Let's do something together.

Let's do something new.

Let's do something fun.

Let's do something silly.

Let's do something adventurous.

Let's do something you like.

Let's do something I like.

Let's do something we both like.

Let's do something just for us.

Let's do it today.

Ode to Valentine's Day

Love is hearts, but not the candy kind.
It's the kind that can be felt and can be
bittersweet. Love can make you queasy, too.

Love is flowers, but not the cut kind.
It's the kind that continues to grow and
blossom. Love never shrivels up and dies.

Love is balloons, but not the helium kind.
It's the kind that has oxygen in it and needs
a gentle, but firm touch to stay up in the air.
Love needs you to breathe into it.

Love is words, but not the kind written by
someone else. It's the kind that can only be
said to you by me and in my own way. Love
is a language understood only by two.

Love is to be celebrated, but not just one
day. It takes a moment to experience and a
lifetime to express. Love changes over the
years, but the wrinkles are laugh lines
instead of frowns. Valentines are good for
one day.

Love is forever.

The House That Love Built
(For Anthony, Alice, Avery, and Alyssa Love)

This is the house that Love built.
A strong house founded on God's Word.
A safe house where the weary find rest.
A loud house with laughter in every room.
A quiet house where prayer and praise
linger in the air.
An open house where friends are always
welcomed.
A spacious house where there is always
room for one more.
A colorful house where creativity brings out the
artist in everyone.
An anointed house where God's hand is
upon all who dwell there.
An appointed house where purpose is
painted on every step.
A blessed house overflowing with God's
favor.
A holy house where the King of Kings pours
out His grace.
This is the house that Love built.
God is Love.

Anniversary Affirmation

I will. Still.
Marry you, go to the ends of the earth
with you, trust you with my life.

I will. Still.
Look at you and want to learn more,
find you sexy, give you all of me.

I will. Still.
Smile when I think of you, look for
your best qualities, thank God for this
divine appointment.

I will. Still.
Love you, believe in you, celebrate the day
we began this journey together.

I will. Still.

Ode to My Cowboy
(for O.C.)

See here I got this cowboy who's right here by my side. In a great big room he became my groom and I became his bride.

He said, *I do* and I said *me too*, though we'd never been on a real date. Then he walked me over the threshold, cuz I was carrying a little extra weight.

Now he's not a man of many words, most times found reading a book. But I knew right away that he knew how to play when he gave me that cowboy look.

And nothing seems a surprise to him or so it seems to me, for his eyes are sharp and his ears are tuned to all activity.

Yet underneath his leather cap and denim dungarees lies a gentle soul with a heart of gold and a will that aims to please.

So come what may we ride together no matter what the days may bring. Cause he's rough and tough with all the right stuff to make this cowgirl sing!

He's my crusty, lusty cowboy with many years out on the range. But deep inside I'm still his bride and that will never change!

When the Sun is Shining

It is the wife who knows her husband.

———

The heart of the wise man lies quiet like limpid water.

———

Wisdom does not come overnight.

———

If you watch your pot, your food will not burn.

—African Proverbs

When the Sun is Shining

When I Love You	31
So Secure ≈	32
Seconds ≈	33
Eating from the Tree	34
Transitions ≈	36

≈ denotes stream poetry

When I Love You

When I love you, its gonna be
like fireworks on the 4th of July with
explosions of color and light.

When I love you, its gonna be
like a star shootin across the sky and lovin
you will be my wish come true.

When I love you, its gonna be
like the sun setting on a crystal lake so
bright and beautiful that I start crying and
don't even know why.

When I love you, its gonna be
like stepping out into space and I'm floating
on air and time seems to stand still.

When I love you, its gonna be
like heaven with lots of singing and
hallelujah shouting and everyday is Sunday

When I love you
When I love you
When I love you
It's gonna be somethin!

So Secure ≈

Here be this Christian woman me walking around on earth with a heavenly smile on my face feelin no shame no pain no disgrace cause me and my man be doin' it yeah I said doin' it and I mean it in every sense of the word and every word of the sense cause hey our love it be so intense that these words I'm telling I just could be yelling for the whole world to hear hey no fear of who might appear to be offended by my blatant rhyme cause I know that it is right on time for us covenant keepers who don't have to play creepers cause we can and do enjoy telling you and you and whoever that we be so secure in our thang walkin talkin connecting on so many levels cause He made us to be one flesh so hey we give it our best we be doin it!

Seconds

You make me greedy for your love
Downright needy for your love
Wanting seconds even with the taste of first
love still in my mouth.

You fill my plate to overflowing like that of
one who has not eaten for many days
And though I am fully satisfied, my mouth
waters for more.

It's just that you taste so good!
Even your smell is an invitation to drink the
fine wine of your lips and dance again to the
rhythm of your hips.
So lead me –feed me – I'm yours.

Eating from the Tree

It wasn't love at first sight it wasn't love that
first night but though I tried with all my
might I soon surrendered willingly.

You didn't woo me, but you really knew me,
touching places in my heart that no other
man had before.

So I gave you all of me nothing left to
mystery you wrote my book with just a look
that made me know- you- were- the one.

You kissed the makeup off my face,
removed my leather and my lace,
you loved me slowly without haste as I said

Yes! Yes to a lifetime with you!

Now the years behind us hold no regret
God says our best hasn't even happened yet
as long as we don't ever let ourselves forget
that it takes three to makes this party last.

Every day has not been fun, but we take
them as they come looking to the future
forgiving the past you- me -and God- it's
already been a blast and I am not tired yet.

So baby keep sweeping me off my feet as we dance to our own beat as we keep making our own heat and enjoying all the treats that only *real* married folks get to eat.

And then... laying side by side like Adam and Eve with nothing to hide we will keep eating from the tree that gives us life.

Transitions ≈

transitions and changes as our life rearranges we stretch and we grow in more ways than we know as we seek hoping to find that one-of-a- kind door that will open just for us so forward we press stopping only to rest but never to give up or give in so we win we win.

When the Rain is Falling

Thunder is not yet rain.

———

Rain does not fall on one roof alone.

———

Don't be so much in love that you can't tell when the rain comes.

———

If the heart is sad tears will flow.

———

Fire and gunpowder do not sleep together.

—African Proverbs

When the Rain is Falling

I Do and You Don't	41
Some of Us Have Rain	42
Not Talking – Day 3	44
Letter from Your Better Half	45
Death by Divorce ≈	46
I'm Gonna Need You Tomorrow ≈	48
Transitions Again!	49

≈ denotes stream poetry

I Do and You Don't

My husband hasn't spoken to me
Since we came home from church.
He from his and I from mine.

But that's not the problem.

I tried to talk to him in the car but he didn't answer. He looked straight ahead with no expression.

But this wasn't the first time.

I used to wonder what I had done wrong. I used to ask him if he was okay. But now I accept his failure to communicate. Only now I realize that this makes me part of the failure when I stop trying.

Our vows are only made good when each one keeps one.

I do and I will both wait expectantly for actions to follow, while you don't and I won't require nothing. So what must we do? Something.

Some of Us Have Rain

Some of us have rain in our houses, while some of us now enjoy sunshine. The rain can come suddenly and without warning, but most of the time, there is ample opportunity to prepare against the storm.

The warning may come as a sudden cool breeze against the face, a gust of wind, a cloudy sky or a rumble of thunder.
The warning speaks to us clearly if we will stop and look up and look around.

It speaks of change. It speaks of change. Change that should come from within our houses before it comes from without.

It speaks of decision. It speaks of decision. Decision to hear and see and prepare even when all looks like fair weather.

It speaks of action. It speaks of action. Action to make change a friend instead of foe. Action that will make decision a delight instead of a dread. Action instead of reaction.

Action that can be instant.
Action that may be constant.

Action that leads to change.
Action that leads to decision,
and more action, and prayer.

Until then, some of us have rain.

Not Talking – Day 3

One day we won't talk again forever.
One day we won't kiss.
One day we won't hug or lay beside each other in bed.
One day we won't have to figure out who said what when and who should apologize first.
One day one of us won't wake up at all and the other one will.
One day there will be no more angry silence and stubborn pride. But there will be silence.
One day there will be no more time for I'm sorry and forgive me.
Someday one day will make all the difference.

Letter from Your Better Half

This is a letter from your wife
This is a letter that can save your life
And our life together.
This letter is written in desperation
Due to our lack of communication
And loss of one accord.
This letter is just one more plea for you to really talk to me
Or you can even write me a letter if that's what it takes for us to get better.
I love you.
Sincerely.
Your wife.

Death by Divorce ≈

Nobody mourns for me the marriage that
was but is no longer to be though once
celebrated with fancy glasses held high now
no last farewell or sad goodbye can be heard
from any who gathered then to wish us well
when our life began together forever till
death us do part because we so loved this
we pledged with our hearts but our hearts
weren't as strong as we once proclaimed or
is it the love that is really to blame for this
breakup and makeup and mix-up and mess
for the months and the years that we now
must confess are a part of our past a
mistake of our youth an error in judgment
but now we know the truth that it takes
more than feelings and words and a ring to
give life to a marriage and to make it lasting
a tie that binds without a pretty pastel bow
but one that while crumpled and dirty will
grow tighter and tighter with the passing of
time will not choke or strangle the life from
the vine that's connected to the tree whose
branches reach high whose roots run deep
so the marriage won't die from the winds
and the rains that are surely to come from
the tests and the trials that will drive you
from home if you let them convince you that

the storm will not cease if you fail to look for answers and settle for release from the moment's affliction and the trial by fire from the day to day struggles from your heart's desire to be one in the flesh a God-given mystery so you sign on the line and we become history.

I'm Gonna Need You Tomorrow ≈

I'm gonna need you tomorrow so don't leave me tonight although we just had a fight and the angry silence is now choking us leaving us breathless and gasping for fresh air and feeling dizzy with the fear that this cloud will never clear and we will never again see the sun shining brightly in our living room and kitchen and bedroom and even in our separate closets that overflow with clothes and shoes and I sure don't want to lose your love so forgive me for whatever I did or said because it all came from my head and not my heart I don't want to be apart from you cause I'm gonna need you tomorrow.

Transitions Again!

Changing, Changing, Ever Changing,
Yet some things remain the same
Stretching, Growing, Seeking, Knowing,
Trusting in that Wondrous Name.

Blue skies, Gray skies, Sunny day skies,
Every season has its own.
Sowing, Reaping, Awake or Sleeping,
Knowing that you are His own.

Praying, Waiting, Consecrating,
Day by day, the Plan unfolds.
Purpose, Vision in each decision
Kept by the One from days of old.

Time to Celebrate Again!

Anticipate the good so that you may enjoy it.

―――

No matter how long the night, the day is sure to come.

―――

If you are building a house and a nail breaks, do you stop building or do you change the nail?

―――

Even the most beautiful fruit may contain a worm.

―――

A wise man who knows his proverbs can reconcile difficulties.

—African Proverbs

Time to Celebrate Again!

Let Us – Renew	55
Love Is…	56
When We Love Someone	57
Looking Forward ≈	58
Our Love for Each Other	60

≈ denotes stream poetry

Let Us – Renew

Let's stay together.
Let's start over.
Let's make it work.
Let's work it out.
Let's try.
Let's try again.
Let's try harder.
Let's think about it.
Let's talk about it.
Let's sleep on it.
Let's pray about it.
Let's seek wise counsel.
Let's ask God.
Let's do it differently.
Let's forgive ourselves.
Let's forgive each other.
Let's trust each other.
Let's be kind to each other.
Let's compliment each other.
Let's look for the good.
Let's be faithful.
Let's win the race.

Love is...

Love is sometimes a hard word but a healing touch.

Love is sometimes a soft word but a sure promise.

Love is sometimes a look that cautions but never kills.

Love is always better than what came before.

Love is to prepare you for what may come.

Love is... God is... love.

When We Love Someone

These things we do when we love someone.
We notice when they breathe differently
even if we say nothing about it.

We feel even the smallest distance between
their heart and ours and we ache with
longing to beat in harmony again.

We make plans to please them in ways that
are special to them, but bring us delight just
by making it happen.

We work to quickly heal from the deepest
cut and the slightest blow, knowing that
love is at the beginning and love will be at
the end.

We tell them over and over again and
we show them over and over and over again
and we inwardly vow to renew our love in at
least a million different ways.

These things we do when we love someone.

Looking Forward ≈

I'm already looking forward to our next anniversary no question as to whether there will be one except for the til death do us part part because I am certain that I want to be with you until then and I'm pretty certain that you feel the same way not because of how we feel today or tomorrow or how we expect to feel next year this time because both of our feelings can surely change between now and then especially mine given my impulsiveness but you know that already because we have a few years under our belt and that means something to us and to God if to nobody else now I find myself smiling as I read in the paper about couples celebrating their 25th or 50th wedding anniversary and I try to imagine what we will look like and how we will be with each other then will you still be as grumpy and will I still be a crybaby or will we both have melted-down together into some processed velveeeta cheese version of who we once were I mean you have already given me your tendency for warts you never told me they were contagious until my first one showed up but with such intimate contact between us we were bound to pass something to each other after all that's how baby got here and we sure want to build on that success and get some others here before the well dries up oh I can here you saying now that you're not going to allow our well to dry up because God has promised that our well will never run dry as long as we trust Him and we know that He is a promise-keeper never falling short of His word you can always count on Him and while that's on my mind I want to tell you that one of the things I love so much about you is that I can always count on you which is just one of the reasons that I am looking forward.

Our Love for Each Other

Our love for each other is God-ordained
Made to take us through storm and rain
Made to keep us when we are weak
And lead us to victory in the face of defeat.
Our love for each other is forged by fire
And strengthened daily by our desire
To prove God's word on which we stand
To taste and see His Holy command,
That from the ground He formed us for each
other that we should prosper and discover
His purpose, His plan through our earthly need
And replenish the earth with Godly seed.
A firm foundation upon which to grow is
what we've been given and seed to sow
So we will let God love us and then love like Him,
you see?
Unconditional, unhindered, forgiving and free.
Our marriage strong, our hearts of flesh,
We give to each other our daily best.
Then this our vow will always be
I do for all eternity.

The Charge

One must talk little and listen much.

———

He who receives a gift does not measure.

———

Unless you call out, who will open the door?

———

When one is in trouble, one remembers God.

———

The ruin of a nation begins in the homes of its people.

—African Proverbs

The Charge to Covenant Keepers
(A ChoreoPoem)

I included this choreographed poem for couples to act out with each other as a way of bonding and play. It confronts issues that many couples may experience to varying degrees: trust, poor communication, shared responsibilities, family relationships, and just plain old everyday annoyances.

As often happens if not addressed, these issues reach a boiling point at the most inconvenient times– like in the middle of the night! There is no putting the problems off any longer – they must be dealt with immediately. While the issues are serious ones, I chose to add a bit of comedy to keep the mood light, while getting the message right! So put on your best acting voice and play children, play!

This Means War!

This Means War!

*Timing and rhyming are crucial to the delivery of the lines, so I **bolded** the rhyming words to assist you.*

Her: Johnny! I just had that dream **again**!

Him: What?

Her: That you and Gina are more than **friends**!

Him: Frankie, this is the 3rd time this **week** that you woke me up out my **sleep**...

Her: I'm just trying to let you **know** that these crazy dreams have got to **go**!

Him: Maybe it's what you eat before you come to **bed** that's putting these silly thoughts in your **head**.

Her: No, it doesn't just happen in the **night**. I'm telling you that something isn't **right**. We don't do the things we used to **do**. And you don't even listen when I talk to **you**. (Pauses) Johnny?

Him: *(Snoring loudly)*

Her: Johnny!

Him: Okay, I'm awake Frankie and it's half past **three**. It sounds like you're

	accusing **me**. But what if I have nightmares of my **own**? About what's happening in our **home**?
Her:	What are you talking about? I'm telling you my **dreams**!
Him:	Frankie, this is bigger than it **seems**. Do you remember last week when I came home **late**, and I got mad because you had locked the **gate**?
Her:	I just forgot – I told you that **then**! Why are you bringing that up **again**?
Him:	And then there are the bills you forget to **pay**. That happens almost every **day**!
Her:	So what? You throw your clothes all over the **floor**. When you use the toilet, you don't even shut the **door**...
Him:	Okay, that's right, let's tell it **all**, like how you check my cell phone **calls**.
Her:	And how you always have something to **do**, when I ask you to take the kids to the **zoo**.
Him:	Your closet filled with bag after **bag** of secret clothes with brand new **tags**!
Her:	The sixty-five inch HD **TV** you bought without consulting **me**!
Him:	Your mama, your daddy and all your **cousins**...

Her: Oh, so now you're trying to play the **dozens**! I know where all this is coming from and I know just what to **do**! I don't have to take this foolishness from **you**!

Him: You're not the only one with a **plan**. I know how I can take a **stand**.

Her: If you're thinking what I'm thinking, then we finally **agree**.

Him: So let's turn on the light, and then we'll just **see**.

(They both stand, and face each other in a "take no prisoners" position.)

Her: I knew it would have to come to **this** when I said my vows and gave you that **kiss**.

Him: I've known for a long time deep **inside**, that this day would come – that we couldn't **hide**.

Her: We should have done this long **ago**, instead of going through this stress and suffering **so**.

Him: We knew the answer was always in our **hands.** We just had our heads stuck in the **sand.** But now it's time...

Her: Johnny, I'm sorry I wasn't more **aware**. I guess we should have spent more time in **prayer**.

Him: Yes, that's the truth, but here we **are**, so...
Both: (shouting) THIS MEANS WAR!
Both: DEVIL hear us! THIS MEANS WAR!
Him: Everything you've taken, every lie you told is **whack**!
The joy we thought was gone forever, we now are getting **back**!
Both: **WAR!**
Her: We know the tricks you play and how you scam and **scheme**!
We know that you are the nightmare, trying to fool us in our **dreams**!
Both: **WAR!**
Him: Our weapons are fully loaded and you- we do not **fear**! No matter what you say or do, we're kicking you out of **here**!
Her: I know my husband is my friend and never my **enemy**! I am flesh of his flesh and bone of his bone, for this was God's **decree**.
Him: Our faith in God and in His Word will always see us **through**, so come what may from day to day,
Both: Devil! You better know we're ready for **YOU**!
THIS MEANS WAR!

love poems for covenant keepers

Before You Go...

Before You Go...

Dear God,
　Thank You for the miracle of marriage. You made it, You designed it, and it is only by You that it will be sustained.
　Thank You for blessing it as a covenant with You so that we could experience this wonderful mystery of becoming one flesh.
　Thank You that, because You are for us, all enemies of our marriage are defeated!
　Thank You for the power of Your Word and Your Spirit to lead us as we take this life journey together.
　We will pray for one another and keep tender hearts towards one another.
　We will forgive ourselves and each other knowing that You forgive us daily.
　We choose to cling to each other when the sun is shining and when the rain is falling.
　We choose to celebrate each other and our life together for as long as we live.
　We do so by faith in the name of Jesus, who saved us and is the Lover of our souls.
　　Amen.

About the PassionWriter

About the PassionWriter

Donna Olds White is described as the PassionWriter because of her early love for writing and speaking words with powerful conviction, which later kindled her love for the spoken word of God. She is refired and refined by her life experiences and what she observes in the lives of others.

I don't take lightly the voice I have as a writer. When I write, I seek to honor our human emotions and experiences and, hopefully, honor God as our Creator.

An artist in several genres, Donna writes poetry, plays, short stories, and songs. She has also created an original twist to traditional poetic forms, dubbing it *stream poetry*™ to describe her free flow of thoughts and emotions. She is also a performance artist, psalmist, community advocate, and workshop facilitator.

Born in Memphis, Tennessee, Donna lives there with her husband and son.

www.ingramcontent.com/pod-product-compliance
Lightning Source LLC
Chambersburg PA
CBHW032212040426
42449CB00005B/560